Sex Addiction

The Ultimate Guide for How to Overcome this Destructive Addiction for Life

I0439770

presentation of the information is without contract or any type of guarantee assurance.

The trademarks that are used are without any consent, and the publication of the trademark is without permission or backing by the trademark owner. All trademarks and brands within this book are for clarifying purposes only and are the owned by the owners themselves, not affiliated with this document.

Table Of Contents

Introduction

Chapter 1: An Overview on Sex Addiction

Chapter 2: How to Overcome Sex Addiction

Chapter 3: Complexities of Sex Addiction

Chapter 4: The Impact on Relationships

Chapter 5: Sex Addiction in the Media and Pop Culture

Conclusion

Introduction

First off, I really want to thank you for downloading this book. The pages in this book were developed through years of experiences that I have gone through, as well as what has proven to work for others that I have talked to and have researched. I also want to congratulate you for taking the time to understand your own sex addiction problem and how you can overcome it.

This book contains proven steps and strategies on how to overcome sex addiction. It discusses a short overview of the addiction, including causes and behavioral patterns, complexities associated to it, impact of the addiction on marriage, and how it is presented in the media and pop culture.

The perception of sexual addiction to many people is skewed because of the lack of respect it receives by those who scrutinize it. However, in this book we will go over why it is often ignored and the staggering statistics of the amount of people who deal with a sexual addiction in their own lives.

This book also features an in-depth explanation on promiscuity as an effect of sex addiction, a sex addict's view on cyberporn, and the so-called "Virgin Sex Addicts". I can guarantee that you will find this book useful if you make sure to implement what you learn in the following pages. The important thing is that you IMPLEMENT what you learn. A sex addiction is not conquered overnight but the important thing to remember is that it is definitely possible for you to overcome it. What I am giving you is the information needed so that you can better understand your own situation, as well as the steps you will need to make that journey.

I recommend that you take notes while you are reading this short book. This will ensure that you get the most out of the information in here. I want you to feel that you made a purchase that is worth your money and I want you to look over the notes of this book even after you've finished reading it. The notes will help you to pinpoint exactly what you need to implement and by writing things down, you will be able to recall specifics and how to handle certain situations when they arise.

Lastly, remember that everything in this book has been compiled through research, my own experiences, as well as the experiences of others, so feel free to question what you have read in this book. I encourage you to do your own research on the things that you want to look deeper into. The more you understand your own past and urges, the better off you'll be. To overcome a sex addiction, it will take some work on your part but you can do it! So remember to read with confidence and an open mind!

Chapter 1:

An Overview on Sex Addiction

Sex addiction (sometimes referred to as Sexual Addiction) is a theoretical model devised to give scientific explanations on sexual thoughts, behaviors, or urges that become extreme or beyond human control. Sex addiction is no longer a new description in literary form, but is known for a number of terms such as: Don Juanitaism, Don Juanism, Satyriasis, Nymphomania, Erotomania, and Hypersexuality.

In 1983, Patrick Carnes popularized the concept of sex addiction through his book. According to Carnes, sex addiction is often associated with obsessive or addictive personalities, self-destructive behavior, low self-esteem, escapism, behavioral conditioning, and other psychological disorders. Hormonal imbalance and alcoholism also affect a person's sexual behavior, as these reduce vital human capacity for intimacy. Addiction, in general, is defined as a person's behavior or state outside the boundaries of norms, which reduces his/her ability to function normally.

Causes of Sex Addiction

Sex addiction is proven by many experts as a phenomenon associated with bipolar disorder, narcissistic personality disorder, and obsessive-compulsive disorder. There are people suffering from more than these three psychological conditions. However, treatment of sex addiction is quite complex, regardless of the gravity of condition. In fact, many clinicians tend to avoid the use of sex addiction diagnosis because of this very fact.

Based on research, many sex addicts show narcissistic behavior, while in some cases, they are believed to show full personality disorders, even after undergoing treatment. Several proponents of studies on the addiction describe it as a person's way of escaping from physical or emotional discomfort through ritualized behaviors such as watching pornographic films, masturbating, and obsessive thoughts. Some sex addicts reconnect themselves with others by showing intimate, impersonal behaviors (exhibitionism, cybersex and voyeurism, to name a few).

Behavioral Patterns

Symptoms of sex addiction may not be decoded easily unless its range of effects become a threat to the addict's personal or social life. Sex is largely important for our species to continue because without sex we can not reproduce. We have developed these sexual urges to keep our species thriving and to ensure reproduction.

But how can we find out if sexual behavior is normal or not? How do we know if our behavior towards sex is healthy or unhealthy? Explained below are eight behavioral patterns indicating sex addiction.

I. *Out-of-Control Sexual Behavior*

Any act associated with sex addiction such as prostitution, exhibitionism, voyeurism, indulging in pornography, and having multiple (or unknown) sexual partners is deemed uncontrollable, especially if the addict increases his/her pleasure upon these acts.

Sexual behaviors that are going beyond the control of the person, are committed regardless of the partner or place. In addition, the sexual intensity arises if the addict considers the act(s) as risk or exploration, which he/she can likely get away with.

II. *Inability to Stop*

The inability to stop sexual acts despite being aware of their consequences is a sign of sexual addiction. Any type of addiction overpowers a person's normal behavior especially if he/she continues to get satisfaction from the desires, despite knowing the consequences.

In sex addiction, the most common consequences are unwanted pregnancies, relationship or marital problems, and health risks (HIV, AIDS, STD etc.).

III. *Ongoing Desire to Limit*

A key sign of addiction is a person's ongoing desire in limiting his/her sexual behavior. When the addict soon realizes the sexual behavior and knowing how wrong it is, he or she will likely escape from the situation by diverting attention to other things. The addict can splurge on material items, move from one house to another, get into a serious relationship, or marry quickly.

IV. *Use of Sex as Self-Destructive Behavior*

An addict's relentless pursuit is to use sex as a way of showing self-destructive behavior. Many sex addicts often say things like "I'll deal with the consequences when I already feel them".

In reality, however, when these consequences are already there, the addict cannot fully redeem his or her self due to moral conflicts, self-hatred, intense levels of anxiety, hopelessness, low self-esteem, and/or humiliation.

V. *Fantasies Or Obsessions As Coping Strategy*

Sex addicts use sexual fantasy, or obsession, as a main coping strategy. Sex addiction usually begins with the simplest acts, including buying pornographic materials. Sooner or later, its frequency (including the desire for searching on some levels that speak of pleasure) worsens the addiction.

The result? The addict will possibly become dissatisfied with his/her sexual fantasies or obsessions. Not to mention, he or she will commit certain overt acts for their own pleasure.

VI. *Mood Changes*

Severe mood changes are often associated with hyper-sexual activity. When the addict cannot develop an emotional attachment to their partner, but instead, gets themselves engaged in risky sexual activities with other people, this causes a mood change because of the games they have to play in their head. If a sex addict is moody, he/she feels the inconsistency and conflicting sides of their emotions, which they cannot control.

VII. *Unwarranted Amount of Time*

An unwarranted amount of time spent in having sex and recovering from it can be the result of a sexual addiction. A sex addict often spends more time engaging themselves in activities that keep them unproductive from work, school, family or even society in general.

VIII. *Neglect of Recreational Activities*

A key sign of sex addiction is the neglect of recreational activities because of sexual activity. Because of sex addiction, the person can no longer set the most important priorities in life (family, school, office duties etc.) that contribute to nurturing self-development.

Chapter 2:

How to Overcome Sex Addiction

In the simplest term, sexual addiction is described as a progressive disorder, characterized by irrational sexual thoughts and acts. Just like other types of addiction, it creates a negative impact not just on the individual, but also to others in their life.

For a number of sex addicts, however, the addiction doesn't only progress to intensified masturbation, or consistent use of the internet and other media to access pornographic materials. For some, the addiction already involves illegal sex activities like rape, obscene phone calls, and child molestation. However, sex addicts do not always eventually become sex offenders. That being said, not all sex offenders are sex addicts.

In a report by Psychcentral, nearly 50% of convicted sex offenders are suffering from the addiction. In the same report, 70% of child molesters are sex addicts. According to a survey conducted by WomanSavers, 64% of women who were molested in their childhood consider the molesters as sex addicts. Statistics like these are clearly an indication that the addiction is a problem that needs more attention.

Consequences of Sex Addiction

The consequences of sex addiction are disturbing not only to the addict, but also to those who are close to him/her. It can leave the person depressed, immensely anxious, or isolated until he/she reaches a point of committing self-harm.

Despair, humiliation, hopelessness, and rejection are among some of the common feelings that a sex addict suffers from.

Ways to Overcome A Sex Addiction

Overcoming a sex addiction can be a bit challenging if you don't have the most useful and safest information at hand. Below is a proven strategy that you or someone close to you can use to overcome a sex addiction:

Accepting

Accept the fact that you are a sex addict. It takes a lot of courage to accept something that others cannot understand. But the truth sets a person free. With acceptance comes the proper initiative in dealing with the problem. The best way to conquer this step is to take a sheet of paper out and write down your feelings about your sexual experiences in the past, as well as what sexual dilemmas you are currently involved in.

Many sex addicts are afraid to admit their problem because they feel that the loved ones in their lives will look down on them. However, sex addiction is one of the few addictions that many people can relate to, even if they don't suffer from it themselves. This is because, often times, the difference between someone with a sex addiction and a person without a sex addiction is just the fact that the person with the addiction has trouble controlling their behavior, although it is common in all humans to think about sex quite often during the day.

Visualizing

Create a visualization of your success by expanding your imagination and seeing yourself overpowering compulsive urges like your sexual behavior. Draw pictures of what your life will be like after you have conquered the sex addiction. Be sure to be as descriptive as possible. By creating this visualization of success, you will have set a goal for what you can work towards in the following steps.

Keep in mind that recovering from sex addiction is completely different from overcoming other forms of dependency. Like other progressive acts showing compulsiveness, one has to figure out what is addictive sex or not. Many see this as a useful tool since it recognizes the sex addict's capacity in knowing what life has to offer that goes beyond the sexual desires.

Focus on other activities that can bring pleasure into your life and find ways to integrate them into your daily schedule. You want as much access to productive activities as possible. For example, lifting weights releases much of the same endorphins that sexual activity does, so focus on working out each day and learn to find pleasure in the process of these natural highs.

Reflect and Forgive

Think and reflect on how much this addiction has changed your life. Take away the power of sex addiction by letting go of the shame or guilt and forgiving yourself, as well as others who were affected by your behavior. This is where many sex addicts struggle and are unable to get over the hump.

The truth is, until you have overcome the shame and guilt associated with your past actions, you will have a hard time letting go of your current thoughts. It is beneficial and recommended to write letters to the people who you feel you have hurt in your past.

Write out deep, emotional letters describing what you feel you have done wrong or what they have done to you. It is up to you whether or not you feel like sending these letters out. Many times, just by writing down these thoughts on paper, you will begin to feel the burden of these problems   disappear.

Addiction Recovery

Participate in addiction recovery programs developed in your community. Sex addiction is obviously an intimacy-related disorder which causes problem not just within yourself, but also for your partner. As a couple, attend therapy/recovery sessions to receive further guidance from the experts. If you are afraid to attend sessions with your partner or if you are single, you can still attend these therapy/recovery sessions by yourself.

These meetings are purposely constructed for people to feel comfortable in. If you are struggling to get up and attend your first meeting, you may feel surprised to know that you would actually feel happier inside the safety of these meetings then you will at home with your emotions bottled up.

Support System

Develop a support system. Just like alcohol and drug addictions, no one deserves to go through the process of breaking an addiction without a support system (which can be your family, friends or work colleagues).

New Behavior

Focus on your new behavior. Recovering from the addiction requires awareness on how your behavior contributes to the addiction. It is also crucial to be mindful of your new set of behaviors and habits (including a visualization of your future goals).

Mindfulness is presented in various forms such as: confiding in those who are closest to you (the ones who care about your success and understand your weaknesses), individual or group counseling, and proper education on sex-related topics.

Some Things to Remember:

To break the cycle of sex addiction, analyzing the root of the problem is important. It is only through this that the addict will be able to seek help from others. To make it to this point, all sex addicts have to go through pain. If that pain caused by the addiction is enough to recognize the underlying issues, then seeking for help and finding solutions to the problem is needed.

Sex addiction has its own roots in molestation. In other words, it is common for a molestation or sex abuse victim to find him or her self reenacting the same pattern from the time that he/she was molested, or exposed to sexual activities. In some cases, the victim won't be able to remember what exactly happened until others will remind him/her.

It creates an impact on relationships. The partner of a sex addict appears to be the most affected in the entire situation. This is because they are unable to comprehend why a person would be addicted to sex, especially if they are unaware of the past influences and events that have happened to their partner.

Hence, when the addict undergoes recovery, his/her partner is in need of help too. In fact, the partner can benefit more from the entire recovery stage because he/she deeply understands what the addict is going through and has enough compassion to help the addict through tough times.

Chapter 3:

Complexities of Sex Addiction

Sex addiction is considered by many as the "most personal" addiction. On the other hand, it is also the most complex.

Overcoming any addiction starts by knowing what and who you're dealing with. However, there are some addictions that don't need to be classified. For example, some alcoholics prefer to drink wine over beer while others will go for anything.

The addictive effect of having intense sexual behavior is diverse. A licensed, comprehensive therapy (i.e. 12-step program on overcoming sex addiction) is not distinguishable between other factors contributing to sex addiction. Most experts use the "Every addiction is just the same" approach. For example, a husband caught cheating on his wife is often advised to use the same modification techniques, especially if the lover is a sex addict.

Virgin Sex Addict – What Is It?

Perhaps you've already heard the term Virgin Sex Addict. The latter is an adult who has never had any sexual experiences with another person, but often masturbates or chronically watches pornographic movies. A virgin sex addict's entire sexual experience is centered on porn addiction and/or curiosity over someone who has had multiple sexual relationships.

According to sex therapists, it looks ridiculous to give a virgin sex addict the same exact treatment as others who are promiscuous.

Promiscuity and Sex Addiction – Are They Different?

An obsession with someone (with a fetish in mind) doesn't result in problems concerning sex addiction. A promiscuous person doesn't have the same addiction as that of the virgin sex addict. The husband or boyfriend cheating on his wife or girlfriend isn't in the same boat as that of the voyeur. Often times, the difference between a promiscuous person and a sex addict is the fact that the promiscuous person may be open with their partners or have open relationships. The person with a sex addiction is usually viewed as the person who keeps it more private or might even lie to their partner in order to have sexual activities behind their back.

Another key difference is that the promiscuous person can control themselves and choose not to ruin relationships or give in to sexual tendencies, while an addict is unable to stop themselves and seems to always end up regretting their decisions.

In overcoming sex addiction, these two factors can be taken into consideration:

Addictive sex alone

This includes masturbation, fantasizing, or any other sexual activity that only requires a single participant.

Addictive sex with others

This includes any type of sexual activity that includes more than one participant.

Psychological Distress Theories in Sex Addiction:

In most of his studies, Carnes argues that children develop "core beliefs" when growing up, based on how their family treats them. According to Carnes, a child coming from a lovable and affectionate family has chances of growing up well, and having faith in others around him/her. A child coming from an unstable or dysfunctional family has chances of growing up developing negative core beliefs – with sex addiction being one of them.

Carnes emphasized in his book these common core beliefs that many sex addicts carry:

"Sex is the most important thing I need."

"My needs will never be met if I depend on others."

"No one will love me for who I am."

"I am nothing, but an unworthy, bad person."

These beliefs drive a person's addiction to sex on its destructive, yet progressive, course presented through the following:

Despair

As the reality of sex addiction worsens, the addict begins to experience humiliation or despair. Oftentimes, he/she experiences feelings closer to betrayal of spiritual perspectives.

Sexual Compulsivity

Here, the tension a sex addict feels is lessened by acting out their sexual intentions. This will make them feel better at certain moments. Compulsivity means that an addict realized that his/her sexual behavior is inevitable, no matter what the consequences or circumstances are.

Altered state of consciousness

Sex addiction is emotionally preoccupied or disconnected from "acting-out" behaviors. This results in a distorted reality perceived by the addict.

Chapter 4:

The Impact on Relationships

According to sex and relationship expert Jerry Kennard, sex addiction is a man's overwhelming desire to have sex. Sexual behavior is considered an addiction when its intensity starts to affect a person's daily living. The "more addictive" the sexual behavior is, the more problems you will face at work, in your personal lifestyle, and even in your relationships with others.

In a recent survey, adults ranging from ages 20–61 experience sexual dysfunction. 40% of women and 50% of men face difficulty in handling sexual behavior. This survey is proof that sex addiction is a major problem in the world today. It is estimated that unnecessary sexual acts affect 4–6% of the United States' population.

Not surprisingly, sex addiction has also become an issue concerning various churches. In some Pentecost churches, seasoned missionaries and youth pastors are using religion to increase their sexual desires. They'll dress up convincingly as church servants, yet they are secretly doing sexual acts with women and children within their congregation.

Impact on Marriage

For most sex addicts, the addiction is more important than career, family, or marriage. They tend to neglect what is most significant in their life, in an attempt to continue protecting their unhealthy sexual acts. A sex addict cannot engage his or her self in a role of being a parent or guardian simply because he/she is dominated by pursuing or focusing on self-defeating sexual acts.

Is Sex Addiction An Excuse For Cheating?

According to Psychcentral, sex addiction is described as a "progressive intimacy condition often characterized by compulsiveness in doing sexual acts or showing pointless sexual behavior". The impact of this addiction in marriage affects not only the couples, but also their children, and it might extend to family members if the addiction worsens.

In a report by the National Council on Compulsivity and Sexual Addiction, a sex addict is defined as "a person engaging in escalating and persistent patterns of sexual behavior that are acted upon despite consequential effects in the society he/she belongs to." In other words, a sex addict who is committed to someone has chances of engaging in sexual activities from other people – no matter how hurtful it will be on his/her partner.

We must realize that if someone suffers from a sex addiction, it is easy to blame them for problems such as a failed marriage or broken relationships, however; after understanding that prior events have a huge influence on current actions, we can see that sex addicts are not consciously choosing to ruin relationships, rather they are just acting out what they subconsciously believe.

Is Sex Addiction Considered A "Real" Addiction?

Sex addiction is an occurrence we often hear nowadays. This has become a subject of jokes or candid humor presented in movies and TV shows. Many people who are unaware of the damage it can bring, dismiss it as one's futile attempt to give some legitimacy to a behavior that is "greedy" or "irresponsible".

Some people say that it happens to those who are unaware of their emotional pain, or have a bizarre perception of sex. If you suffer from a sex addiction, do not let these outside ideas get to you and your path to recovery. Remember that people who do not suffer from a sex addiction will have trouble ever understanding your point of view so don't waste your time getting angry if a person can not accept your viewpoint.

Chapter 5:

Sex Addiction In the Media and Pop Culture

Sex addiction became a hot topic in the media after actor David Duchovny admitted publicly that he was a sex addict and needed to undergo months of rehabilitation in 2009. The X-Files star was then happily married to actress Tea Leoni. They even have children named Madeline West and Kyd Miller.

The World Wide Web continues to deal with issues surrounding the unprecedented number of pornographic materials being accessed by everyone. Many internet users get bombarded with websites showing pop-up messages, or advertisements of sex websites. Because of this, even children and teenagers now have access to various pornographic sites. The nature of online pornography makes it challenging for lawmakers to trace each individual's activity or place limits on internet use.

Is Cyberporn Viewing Considered Sex Addiction?

Compulsive viewing of the so-called Cyber Pornography or Cyberporn creates behavioral patterns that are similar to liquor and drug addiction, according to Carnes. This involves a person acting on uncontrollable sexual behaviors such as having inconsistent affairs with strangers, compulsive masturbation, and continuous viewing of pornographic films online.

The sex addict will likely experience consequences such as loss of work opportunities, relationship/marital problems, and exposure to sexually-related diseases. Most online pornography addicts slowly increase their satisfaction with sex by seeking unusual sexual experiences and watching more intense online pornography.

In a study conducted by San Jose Marital & Sexuality Clinic, almost 80% of adolescents use the computer for cyberporn viewing and other sex-related purposes. In addition, nearly 2–4% of these adolescents are classified as sex addicts.

Sex Addiction in Movies

Sex addiction is also presented in a number of movies. One of which is Don Jon, a story about a young, handsome, and charismatic man who is a sex addict by nature. The film was written by Joseph Gordon-Levitt in 2008.

Other movies with sex addiction as the main theme are:

Lolita

Based from Vladimir Nabokov's 1955 novel of the same name, the movie tells the story of a middle-aged professor's sexual obsession with a 12-year old girl.

Shame

A British comedy–drama directed by Steve McQueen, Shame tells the story of a successful advertising executive's dark secret, which is his sex addiction.

Spanking The Monkey

A 1994 comedy film about a sexual relationship between two siblings, the film also tackled issues on incest and teenage liberalism.

Kissed

The 1996 Canadian film written and directed by Lynne Stopkewitch is based on a short story by Barbara Gowdy. It chronicles the story of a young woman and her sexual obsession with a dead man.

Crash

The 1966 psychological thriller directed by David Chronenberg is based on a novel by J.G Ballard. The film's portrayal of sex addiction and violence stirred criticism, which resulted in it being banned in some countries. Crash won the Jury Prize at the Cannes Film Festival in 1996 and earned a Golden Palm nomination at the same event.

Conclusion

I worked hard on creating the best guide for "overcoming a sex addiction" that I could. Sex addiction stops many people from accomplishing things in their lives because of self-esteem and trust issues. These are all the strategies and information that have worked for me, as well as others that I have talked to and researched. I guarantee if you stay consistent they will work for you as well. Be optimistic about your current situation and make small progress each day!

I hope this book will be a tool to help you recover from sex addiction. I also hope that this book was able to help you to get a deeper understanding of the effects of indulging in pornography, voyeurism and other related activities that trigger needless sexual behavior.

The next step is to go back through the book and your notes, and follow each recovery technique, and reflect on the consequences and impact of sex addiction not just to you, but also to your family and friends. Be sure to take ACTION on these steps in order to see results. Remember, the only way to see massive results is by taking massive action.

If you feel like you learned something from this book, please take the time to share your thoughts with me by sending me a message. I would also appreciate it if you left a review on Amazon.

Thank you and good luck in your journey!